T0398466

EN
construcción

Construction
SITE

LAS RETRO-EXCAVADORAS
BACKHOES

Dan Osier

Traducción al español: Eida de la Vega

PowerKiDS press

New York

Published in 2014 by The Rosen Publishing Group, Inc.
29 East 21st Street, New York, NY 10010

First Edition

Editor: Amelie von Zumbusch
Book Design: Andrew Povolny

Traducción al español: Eida de la Vega

Photo Credits: Cover iStockphoto/Thinkstock; p. 5 pryzmat/shutterstock.com; pp. 7, 13, 17, 21, 23 Dmitry Kalinovsky/shutterstock.com; p. 9 Hemera/Thinkstock; p. 11 Photodisc/Thinkstock; p, 15 a-poselenov/shutterstock.com; p. 19 Joseph Nettis/Photo Researchers/Getty Images.

Library of Congress Cataloging-in-Publication Data

Osier, Dan.
  Backhoes = Las retroexcavadoras / by Dan Osier ; translated by Eida de la Vega. — First edition.
     pages cm. — (Construction site = En construcción)
  Includes bibliographical references and index.
  ISBN 978-1-4777-3286-1 (library)
  1. Backhoes—Juvenile literature. I. Osier, Dan. Backhoes. II. Osier, Dan. Backhoes. Spanish. III. Title. IV. Title: Las Retroexcavadoras.
  TA735.O8518 2014
  629.225—dc23

                                 2013022462

Websites: Due to the changing nature of Internet links, PowerKids Press has developed an online list of websites related to the subject of this book. This site is updated regularly. Please use this link to access the list: www.powerkidslinks.com/cs/backho/

Manufactured in the United States of America

CPSIA Compliance Information: W14PK3: For Further Information contact Rosen Publishing, New York, New York at 1-800-237-9932

Contenido

Contents

Las retroexcavadoras son útiles. Con ellas, se puede cavar y transportar tierra.

Backhoes are useful. People dig and move dirt with them.

4

La palabra "retroexcavadora" viene de "retroceder" y "excavadora".

The word "backhoe" is short for "backhoe loader."

7

Su nombre viene de la forma en que arrastra la tierra hacia sí cuando cava.

Backhoes got their name because they draw dirt back toward themselves.

8

9

Las primeras se hicieron en Inglaterra.

The first ones were made in England.

El cargador está al frente.
Se usa para cargar cosas.

The loader is in the front. It is used to carry things.

12

La cuchara se usa para cavar. Está detrás.

The bucket is used for digging. It is in the back.

15

El brazo y la pluma conectan la cuchara al tractor.

The **stick** and **boom** connect the bucket to the tractor.

17

El **operador** se sienta en la cabina del tractor.

The **operator** sits in the tractor's cab.

18

19

Muchos operadores de retroexcavadoras trabajan para compañías de construcción. Otros trabajan para pueblos o en granjas.

Most backhoe operators work for construction companies. Others work for towns or on farms.

20

21

Es divertido ver funcionar una retroexcavadora.
¿Has visto una alguna vez?

It is fun to watch a backhoe at work. Have you ever seen one?